01019I3

JBIOG
Colum 01-15-09
Larkin, Tanya

Christopher Columbus

Christopher Columbus

Tanya Larkin

The Rosen Publishing Group's
PowerKids Press™
New York

For Mrs. Metzger of St. Jerome's Elementary School
Philadelphia, Pennsylvania

Published in 2001 by The Rosen Publishing Group, Inc.
29 East 21st Street, New York, NY 10010

Photo Credits: Cover and title page, pp. 8, 15 © Archive Photos; p. 2 © Art Resource; pp. 4, 8, 15, 16, 11, 19, 20 © Northwind; p. 1, 2, 3, 4, 7, 11, 12, 19, 20 © Granger Collection.

First Edition

Book Design: Maria E. Melendez and Felicity Erwin

Larkin, Tanya.
    Christopher Columbus / Tanya Larkin— 1st ed.
        p. cm.— (Famous explorers. Set 1)
    Includes index.
    Summary: Brief text and illustrations chronicle the life, voyages, and discoveries of the intrepid explorer.
    ISBN: 0-8239-5554-0 (lib. bdg. : alk. paper)
    1. Columbus, Christopher—Juvenile literature. 2. America—Discovery and exploration—Spanish—Juvenile literature. 3. Explorers—Spain—Biography—Juvenile literature. 4. Explorers—America—Biography—Juvenile literature. [1. Columbus, Christopher. 2. Explorers. 3. America—Discovery and exploration—Spanish.] I. Title. II. Series.

E111 .L37 2000
970.01'5'092—dc21
[B]   00-020249

Manufactured in the United States of America

Contents

4

Born With a Mission

Christopher Columbus was born in Genoa, Italy, in 1451. His parents named him after Saint Christopher, the **protector** of travelers. This name means someone who brings the story of Christ to other people. Having this name made Christopher Columbus believe he was chosen by God to travel the world and spread Christianity. Columbus wanted to meet the emperor of China and **convert** him and his people to Christianity. When Christopher was young, little did he know where his desire to spread his religion would lead him. He would become one of the greatest explorers of all time.

Christopher Columbus was named for Saint Christopher (at left). Many trading ships sailed from Columbus's hometown, Genoa.

A Natural Sailor

When Columbus was about 14, he sailed from Genoa, Italy, to other cities by way of the Mediterranean Sea. He went on these journeys to trade goods. Columbus discovered that he had a special talent for **navigation**. He always knew how to find the right wind to push the ship forward. There is a story that says that during one of these trips, pirates attacked his ship. Columbus swam to shore and found himself in another European country called Portugal. Portugal had the best sailors and explorers in the world. It was there that Columbus decided to search for the quickest **route** to the Indies.

Columbus was a skilled sailor and navigator. He often traveled on ships like this one.

Portugal

7

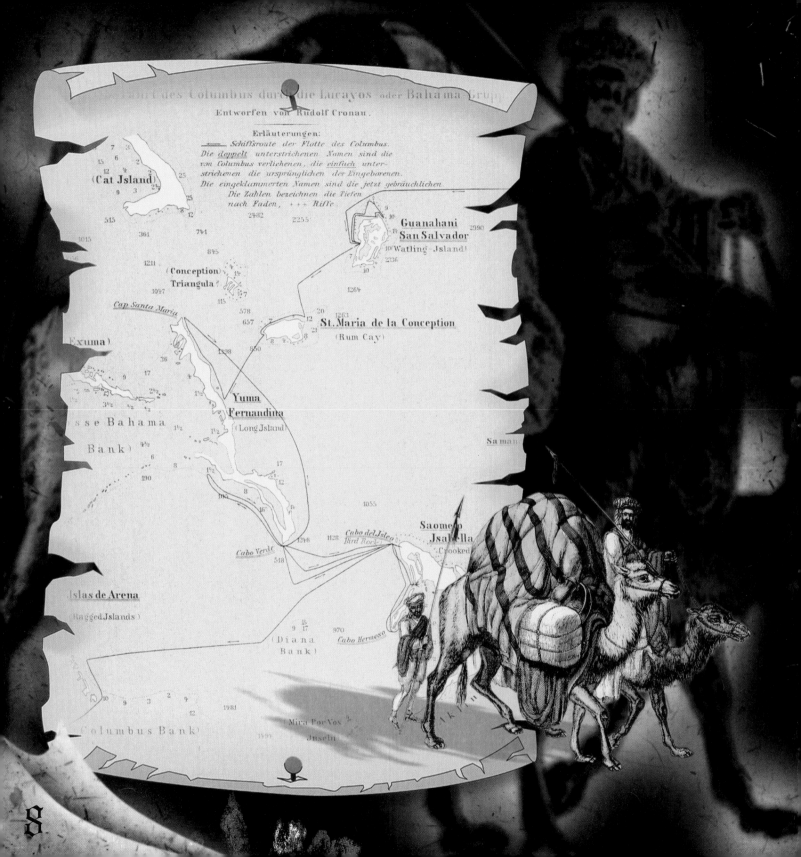

Fahrtdes Columbus durch die Lucayos oder Bahama Gruppe

Entworfen von Rudolf Cronau.

(Cat Jsland)

Guanahani
San Salvador
(Watling-Jsland)

(Conception)
Triangula

Cap Santa Maria

St. Maria de la Conception
(Rum Cay)

Exuma)

Yuma
Fernandina
(Long Jsland)

sse Bahama

Bank)

Saman

Saometo
Jsabella
(Crooked

Cabo del Jsleo
Bird Rock

Cabo Verde

Islas de Arena

(Ragged Jslands)

(Diana
Bank)

Cabo Hermoso

(Columbus Bank)

Mira Por Vos
Jnseln

8

The Race to the Indies

Europeans were eager to find a quick and easy route to the area they called the Indies. The Indies was the name given to the land of and around China, Japan, and India. European traders crossed many deserts to get to the Indies by land. This was a long, hard trip. Europeans wanted to find a faster, easier way to get to the region that had so many valuable goods. Many sailors from Portugal wanted to sail east around the tip of Africa. Columbus believed there was a shorter way. The maps he studied made it look like he could reach the Indies by sailing west across what we now call the Atlantic Ocean. Even though others disagreed, Columbus believed that the world was small and that the voyage across the Atlantic would be short.

Columbus sailed through islands called the Bahamas in the Americas. He thought he had reached the Indies.

Rejection and Hope

Explorers in the 1400s needed to find patrons, or people who would give them money and supplies for their trips. Columbus asked King John II of Portugal for ships and supplies for his trip. The king wouldn't give these things to the young explorer. Columbus felt **frustrated**, but never gave up hope. He believed that God had a plan for his future. He went to Spain to talk to King Ferdinand and Queen Isabella. He hoped they would support his voyage. After many years he convinced Spain's king and queen to help. He told them that his trip would cost them very little compared to all the gold he would bring back from the Indies.

Columbus needed help to make a voyage to the Indies. Other sailors helped him plan the journey (above). King Ferdinand and Queen Isabella of Spain gave him money (below).

SPAIN

11

The Nina, the Pinta, and the Santa Maria

King Ferdinand and Queen Isabella ordered the people of Palos, Spain, to give Columbus three wooden ships. The *Santa Maria* was a kind of ship called a **nao**. It was about 117 feet (36 meters) long. The *Nina* and *Pinta* were called **caravels**. They were about half as long as the nao. Each ship had large and small sails for better sailing. The ships were also loaded with guns for self-defense. Columbus brought many different kinds of people with him on these ships. There was an **interpreter**, who could speak with the Chinese emperor, a doctor, a record keeper, a **scribe**, and many **gromets**. Gromets were young boys who cooked meals and kept track of time by turning an **hourglass**.

The Santa Maria was the largest and slowest of the three ships. The Nina was the smallest, and the Pinta was the fastest.

The Reward

As soon as Columbus's ships left Spain in August 1492, the **crew** began to panic. The water seemed to stretch on forever. The crew members were afraid they would be lost at sea. Some sailors threatened to kill Columbus if he did not turn back. To calm his sailors, Columbus reminded them of the reward Queen Isabella had promised to give to the first person who spotted land. Soon the sailors began to see signs of land. They saw birds, seaweed, and sticks floating in the water. On October 12, 1492, a sailor yelled "Land! Land!" Columbus said that he saw the land first. The other sailor did not get the reward.

Columbus left Spain on August 3, 1492. On October 12, he reached the New World.

16

Two Worlds Meet

As the *Nina*, the *Pinta*, and the *Santa Maria* approached the shore, people swam out to the ships to greet the newcomers. Columbus called these people Indians because he thought that he had landed close to the Indies. We now know that they were a group of Native Americans called Arawaks. The Native Americans gave the Europeans parrots, cotton, and hunting spears. Columbus gave them **trinkets**, like glass beads, brass rings, and bells. He saw that they had gold rings in their noses and asked them where he could find more gold. They showed him a stream with gold flakes in it. Columbus was not satisfied. He needed to find more than just flakes to impress the king and queen of Spain.

Native Americans gave food to Columbus's shipwrecked crew. In return Columbus gave them bells and other trinkets.

Slaves Instead of Gold

Columbus **claimed** the island for the king and queen of Spain. He named it San Salvador. The area where the crew landed is now known as the West Indies. When he left San Salvador, he decided to take some of the Arawaks with him. Columbus needed to bring the king and queen something to prove his trip was a success. This way they would give him more supplies for future trips. He thought he could turn the Arawaks into **slaves**. He knew the king and queen would like having the Arawaks work for free. He also would be able to teach the Indians about Christianity. He thought it was in their best interest to learn about Christianity. Today we know that people should not be forced to be slaves or to accept other people's religious beliefs.

Columbus landed in the Bahamas on an island he named San Salvador. He made slaves of the people there and took them back to Spain.

A Ship Turned Into a Fort

Before sailing home, Columbus wanted to search for more gold. The crew still thought they were near the Indies, so they sailed from harbor to harbor looking for riches. The *Santa Maria* tore its bottom on a rock near the island we now call the Dominican Republic. Columbus built a fort on the island from the boards of the wrecked ship. He called the fort Navidad, which is the Spanish word for Christmas. Columbus gave the fort this name because the shipwreck happened on Christmas Eve. When Columbus returned to Navidad on his second voyage about a year later, he found dead bodies everywhere. The Spaniards he had left in charge of the fort had treated the Native Americans badly. The Native Americans had **rebelled**.

The Santa Maria was a ship in the fleet that Columbus took to the New World. Once they arrived on land, the crew mistreated the people who were already living there.

21

The Trickster

In 1504, Columbus was **stranded** on an island. The people there would not feed his hungry crew. Columbus tricked the people. He knew an **eclipse** was coming. He told the people that God sent the eclipse to eat the moon. This scared them into giving his crew food. A year later a ship brought the crew back to Spain. While he had not reached the place he had hoped, Columbus was among the first Europeans to reach the Americas. He died on May 20, 1506, at home in Spain.

Columbus's Timeline

1450s-Columbus grows up in Genoa, Italy.

1460s-Columbus goes to work on trading ships.

1484-Columbus asks King Ferdinand and Queen Isabella of Spain for money to go to the Indies.

1492-Columbus sets sail for the Indies. He arrives in the Americas.

Glossary

caravels (KAR-uh-vels) Ships used in the 1400s that were powered by sails.

claimed (KLAYMD) To have taken something and then say it belongs to the person who took it.

convert (kuhn-VERT) To change religious beliefs.

crew (KROO) A group of sailors that work on the same ship.

eclipse (EE-klips) When the sun covers the moon so that it looks like the moon has disappeared.

frustrated (FRUS-tray-ted) Feeling angry or sad because you cannot do anything about a certain situation.

gromets (GRAH-mets) Young boys on the ship's crew who cooked and kept track of time.

hourglass (OW-er-glas) An instrument used to measure time with sand, mercury, or water.

interpreter (in-TER-prih-ter) Someone who helps people who speak different languages talk to each other.

nao (NYOW) A medium-sized sailing ship of the late 1400s.

navigation (na-vuh-GAY-shun) The art of knowing how to get from one place to another.

protector (pruh-TEK-ter) Someone who keeps others from harm.

rebelled (ruh-BELD) To have disobeyed the people or country in charge.

route (ROOT) The path you take to get somewhere.

scribe (SKRYB) A person whose job it is to copy books by hand.

slaves (SLAYVS) People who are owned by another person and are forced to work for him or her.

stranded (STRAN-did) To be left alone in a scary or hard situation.

trinkets (TRINK-its) Small cheap objects.

Index

Web Sites

To learn more about Christopher Columbus, check out this Web
site: www1.minn.net/~keithp/